PRAISE FOR THE WORKS OF JUAN GELMAN

T0161515

"How fortunate that Hardie St. Martin, an exemplary translator of Spanish-language poetry, a tutelary spirit to so many poet/transla-tors, turned his deep attention to Juan Gelman, an Argentinean poet who connects beauty to justice. . . . Gelman is an unwavering poet of conscience—his work is dedicated to the Disappeared—but his lamentations keep giving way to praise of the renewable world. This book, a collaboration of spirits, is a testament to the way that poetry expresses what would otherwise be inexpressible."

—Edward Hirsch

"Perhaps the most admirable element of Gelman's poetry is the un-thinkable tenderness he shows . . . calling upon so many shadows for one voice to lull and comfort, a permanent caress of words on unknown tombs."

—Julio Cortázar

"Juan Gelman does not imitate the tango; he contains it."

—Eduardo Galeano

"Gelman's poetry is epic in its scope—no corner of life goes unnoticed in this work. . . . Rendered in a breathless style, this is the diary of a human heart in a rough world where artistry is the first salvation."

—Oscar Hijuelos

DARK TIMES
FILLED
WITH LIGHT

THE SELECTED
WORK OF
JUAN GELMAN

Translated from the Spanish by Hardie St. Martin
Introduction by Paul Pines

OPEN LETTER
LITERARY TRANSLATIONS FROM THE UNIVERSITY OF ROCHESTER

First edition, 2012
Second edition, 2023

Poems from this collection have appeared in the following: Juan Gelman Tribute
Issue of the *Café Review*, Summer 2009; *Exquisite Corpse*, January 11, 2011:
"Gotán," "He Was Born on the Edge of a Disastrous Day," "Alone," "Saint Theresa";
Big Bridge #15, Spring 2011: "One Man's Wake," "A Woman and a Man,"
"For the Time Being," "Hymn of Victory," "Courage," "Snows,"
"Commentary xix," "Other Writings," "Rain," "Faithless," "The Banished,"
"On Learning That My Enemy Had Died," "xvii," "At Daybreak," "The Animal."

Library of Congress Cataloging-in-Publication Data:

Gelman, Juan, 1930–
    [Selections. English]
    Dark times filled with light : the selected work of Juan Gelman / by Juan Gelman ;
  translated from the Spanish by Hardie St. Martin. — 1st ed.
      p. cm.
    Includes bibliographical references.
    ISBN-13: 978-1-934824-68-9 (pbk. : acid-free paper)
    ISBN-10: 1-934824-68-2 (pbk. : acid-free paper)
    I. St. Martin, Hardie. II. Title.
    PQ7797.G386A6 2013
    861'.64—dc23
                      2012022672

Text set in Chaparral.

Design by N. J. Furl

Open Letter is the University of Rochester's nonprofit, literary translation press:
Lattimore Hall 411, Box 270082, Rochester, NY 14627

www.openletterbooks.org

CONTENTS

DARK TIMES FILLED WITH LIGHT:
AN INTRODUCTION

This collection of poetry presents the selected work of a living master, the Argentine poet Juan Gelman, translated by the late Hardie St. Martin. Virtually unknown in English literary circles and the recipient of the highest literary honors in the Spanish-speaking world, Gelman is on the short list of Nobel Prize candidates.

Juan Gelman was born in Buenos Aires in 1930 to a father who had participated in the 1905 Russian revolution before immigrating to Argentina. Juan was a political activist until the 1976 Argentine coup d'état brought a reign of terror to Buenos Aires. Gelman's son, Marcelo, and daughter-in-law, Claudia, pregnant with the poet's grandchild, were "disappeared." The poet spent the next thirty years as an exile in Mexico and Europe. In 2000, after decades of searching, he located his granddaughter, born before her mother's murder and given to a pro-government family in Uruguay.

The Argentina that nurtured the tango, and then "disappeared" its people, became the crucible for a poet. Steeped in the authority of his wound, Gelman's poems transform the unspeakable into an affirmation that locates light even in the darkest of times:

dark times / filled with light / the sun

spreads sunlight over the city split

by sudden sirens / the police hunt goes on / night falls and we'll

make love under this roof . . .

What a daunting task it must have been for St. Martin to find in his own depth the resources that allowed him to touch the source of Gelman's vision and render it whole. As Nietzsche reminds us, when you look into the abyss, the abyss looks into you.

THE TEST OF TRUTH

Hardie St. Martin schooled a generation of poet/translators including Robert Bly, James Wright, Jonathan Cohen, and David Unger. His 1975 anthology of 20th century Spanish poetry, *Roots & Wings*, was hailed as "a landmark" by *Kirkus Reviews*. In his long career he translated work by Vicente Aleixandre, Roque Dalton, José Donoso, Blas de Otero, Nicanor Parra, Luisa Valenzuela, and Pablo Neruda, among others. St. Martin died in Barcelona in September of 2007. His focus on Gelman's poems was ongoing during the last years of his life; he regarded it as the jewel in the crown of his achievements. A year before he died, after plans to publish the book failed to materialize, St. Martin forwarded the files containing the poems and his notes to me.

On reading the translations, my eyes snapped open. I was reminded of why I was first drawn to poetry, and haunted by what I found. St. Martin's renderings of Gelman's poems stood what George Oppen calls "the test of truth," which leaves no room for pretension or dissimulation. A true translation isn't about the substitution of words, but the alignment of symmetries under the verbal radar. A poet of Gelman's depth can speak the dead back to life. Both the original poem and the translation must deal with the voices of the dead as facts.

one day i watched death going by / she wasn't on horseback / she
    was screaming

. . .

this one was screaming like one of the damned / of no help to her
the lovely summer the fountains the women she allowed to go on
    their way

St. Martin understood that the translation must touch the emotion
at its origin. He located that point in Gelman's fascination with the
16th century poet and mystic, San Juan de la Cruz, who used the
language of loss to approach divine love through what he called "the
dark night of the soul." St. Martin reflected Gelman's courage at the
edge of the abyss.

A Knowing Beyond Knowledge

Following in the footsteps of San Juan, Gelman abandoned himself
to the ache of a secular compassion: "my soul passed through like a
voice/ walking now with the world's feet." This journey strips bare all
who take it. Any hope the civilized Ego carries with it is left at the
door. Gelman speaks of a "lenguaje calcinado," as it refers to a dis-
calced (barefoot) poetry. The word was used by San Juan to describe
his own stripped down poetic lines, and the monastic reforms he
brought to his order of Discalced Carmelites. Only barefoot poetry
can express what so many have suffered at the hands of despots.

        Like a hard taskmaster
        it makes me work day and night,
        in pain, in love,

out in the rain, in dark times,

when tenderness or the soul opens its arms,

when illness weighs down my hands.

In his notes on the manuscript, St. Martin writes: Comentarios—
tormented language of the soul tortured by divine love . . . echoes St.
John . . . puts the saint's methods to his own use.

For San Juan and Gelman, a discalced language is a finger point-
ing at a landscape without a vanishing point. We enter a dimension
beyond rational experience to face the deeper consciousness left to
us when all else is stripped away, and gives us poems that reach out
from the "cloud of unknowing" and open the heart to what the mind
can't bear.

move up closer to me / sadness / so

much anger and so many dead ports

send a chill through me but

i have to go on moving / on and on

In his own dark night of the soul, Gelman finds sufficient light to
express the inexpressible—which is why the Argentine poet Juan
Daniel Perrotta calls him "the icon of the nation's pain" and "the voice
of those who can't be heard." Gelman describes this state of mind in
his *Commentary II* as one that "makes me childish like feet crushing/
sadnesses on the edge of what it is about to sing . . ."

In the embrace of unknowing, we rediscover what is most humane
in what had seemed an irredeemable world of loss and isolation. In
"An Open Letter To My Son" the poet states:

crestfallen my burning soul

. . .

opens its breast to take you in /

protect you / reunite you / undie you /
your little shoe stepping on the

. . .

world's suffering softening it /

"There are losses," says Gelman. "The important thing is how return-
ing to them transforms them into something new."

Of Exile

An interviewer once said to Gelman: "In your writings, the universe
manifests itself through written signs [historical narrative]; as though
all activity could be transformed into writing." To this Gelman re-
sponded: "The universe writes from the depth and breadth of time.
Miserable and poor is the human being who never gets to read that
writing."

What transforms those of us who read that writing may be our
willingness to enter the valley of the shadow, a walk we take alone,
as exiles stripped of everything that defined us. Gelman is not only
an exile from Argentina, but like San Juan a grandchild of conversos,
an exile from his Jewish roots. As Gelman puts it: "I was never the
owner of my own ashes, obscure faces write my verses . . ."

The loss of ancestors, family and children drove Job to question
the whirlwind. When he asks, "Why?" God answers him with the
dimensions of the firmament that transform his outrage into a will-
ing incomprehension. What Gelman admires most in San Juan, is his
idea of "knowing through not knowing." But the Argentine poet goes
beyond mystic paradox in his willingness to heal the pain of exile and
loss by holding it in the vessel of an open heart.

St. Martin, too, was an exile; of Guatemalan and Belizean parent-
age, he was never at home in either country, nor in his ancestral lands

in Monkey River. As a gunnery officer in WWII, he lost his hearing in one ear. He was socially awkward in bohemian circles and even more so in academic ones, which he found stuffy. The closest place he found to a home was his apartment not far from the Ramblas district of Barcelona, during his last decade, and in Gelman's work. The result is the remarkable book that follows.

END NOTES

St. Martin's files remained on my computer unknown to anyone but Guatemalan novelist and translator David Unger, until Steve Luttrell, editor of *The Café Review*, asked if I'd edit a tribute to Juan Gelman for the Summer 2009 issue. The opportunity helped to bring what had been hidden in my files to light.

This selected work, as conceived by St. Martin, spans the years from 1956 to 1992. The collections represented are listed in chronological order. Common to Gelman's oeuvre are series attributed to personas such as John Wendell and Yamanocuchi. "Citations" and "Commentaries" are addressed to Gelman's significators, San Juan de la Cruz and Santa Theresa de Jesus. "Com/positions" are Gelman's versions of 10th/11th century Sephardic poets with whom he shares the experience of violence and exile, and are "tenants of the same condition . . . who offer me the past, surround my present and give me a future." In his prologue to these poems, St. Martin states: ". . . translation is something inhuman: no language or face lets itself be translated. You have to leave one beauty intact and supply another to go with it: their lost unity lies ahead." St. Martin's translations arrive splendidly with Gelman at that destination.

Paul Pines
2012

DARK TIMES
FILLED
WITH LIGHT

FROM
VIOLIN AND OTHER QUESTIONS
(1956)

WATCHING PEOPLE WALK ALONG

Watching people walk along, put on a suit,
a hat, an expression and a smile,
watching them bent over their plates eating patiently,
work hard, run, suffer, cringe in pain,
all just for a little peace and happiness,
watching people, I say it's hardly fair
to punish their bones and their hopes
or distort their songs or darken their day,
                            yes, watching
people weep in the most hidden corners
of the soul and still be able
to laugh and walk with dignity,
watching people, well, watching them
have children and hope and always
believe things will get better
and seeing them fight to stay alive,
                            I tell them,
it's beautiful to walk along with you
to discover the source of new things,
to get at the root of happiness,
to bring the future in on our backs, to address
time on familiar terms and know
we'll end up finding lasting happiness,
I tell them, it's beautiful, what a great mystery
to live treated like dirt
                    yet sing and laugh,
                            how strange!

FROM
THE NAME OF THE GAME
(1956–1958)

I SIT HERE LIKE AN INVALID

I sit here like an invalid in the desert of my desire for you.

I've grown used to sipping the night slowly, knowing
you're in it somewhere filling it with dreams.

The night wind whips the stars flickering in my hands,
broken-hearted widows of your hair, still unreconciled.

The birds you planted in my heart are stirring and
sometimes with a knife's cold blade
I'd offer them the freedom they demand to go back to you.

And yet I can't. You're so much a part of me, so much alive in me
that if I died, my death would kill you.

STRIKE AT THE CONSTRUCTION SITE

Neither the strong noon wine
they'd drink out in the wind.
Nor the ladder, the sun, the air.
Silence stands on the scaffolding.

The men looked at one another patiently
from the heart straight to the bone.
They touched death further down.
And they made up their minds.

Maybe maría'll cry over these things
and she'll do it secretly.
She'll have to dry her cheeks with the night.
Her man won't know it, one less worry for him.

The man will stare at his quiet hands,
he'll either say I have or I don't have.
He'll grow from his balls on up,
made pure once again.

Pure now that there's wine in his brother,
small pieces of bread in pedro's eyes.
And on the strength of this
the child in his heart comes back again.

And on the strength of this
the silence on the scaffolding
takes its hat off to him.

FROM
ONE MAN'S WAKE
(1961)

ONE MAN'S WAKE

He goes around concerned more than usual
about time, life, other minor things like being,
dying without having found himself.

He was single-minded about this and on rainy days
he would go out and start asking if they had seen him
aboard some woman's eyes or somewhere along
the Brazilian coast in love with its pounding surf
or most likely at the funeral of his innocence.

He always had words or pale and miserable pieces
of love and of violent winds in reserve,
he had been about to enter death thirteen times
but came back from force of habit, he said.

Among other things he wanted
someone else to understand the world
and this terrified loneliness itself.

Now they're holding this scary wake here
inside these walls on which his curses still come rolling off,
the rustle of his beard, still full of life, falls from his face
and no one who can smell him
will ever guess how much he wanted to enjoy the mystery of
    innocent love
and give water to his children.

As he returns his borrowed skin and bones to neglect,
he makes out his own figure in the distance and runs after himself,
so there's no doubt now
that it will soon begin to rain.

THE ART OF POETRY

Of all trades, I've chosen one that isn't mine.

Like a hard taskmaster
it makes me work day and night,
in pain, in love,
out in the rain, in dark times,
when tenderness or the soul opens its arms,
when illness weighs down my hands.

The grief of others, tears,
handkerchiefs raised in greeting,
promises in the middle of autumn or fire,
kisses of reunion or goodbye,
everything makes me work with words, with blood.

I've never been the owner of my ashes, my poems,
obscure faces write my verses like bullets firing at death.

WINTER

After making love
your skin still lights the darkness, the weariness,
the night taking shelter in this room.

The silence has shivered for us
like the naked feet of this winter of the poor,
faces love left behind still linger in your arms,
we make our way back to the fire, the anger, the injustice
after making love.

In this city moaning like a madwoman
love quietly counts
the birds that died fighting the cold,
the jails, the kisses, the loneliness, the days
still left before the revolution.

THE THIEF

In the night, so dark and quiet,
shying away from everything human or animal,
secretly, without a sound, he steals
fire from words and words from fire
for himself, for everyone, for the love he'll never know.
The cold ashes punish his hands.

THE GIRL ON THE BALCONY

The afternoon went down that street near the port
making its way slowly, swaying, filled with odors.
The old houses look pale on afternoons like this,
their squalid sadness shows more than ever and their walls
look unhappier than usual, deep stairways
give off light like phosphorescence from the sea
and perhaps dead eyes watch the late afternoon as if remembering.

It was six o'clock, something gentle stopped the newcomers,
something gentle as if coming from the afternoon's lips,
                    something full of lust.
Faces relax on afternoons like this,
they burn with something childlike
against the darkness, the breath of dancehalls.

This gentleness was as if each one were remembering a woman,
their thighs intertwined, his head on her belly,
the silence of the newcomers
was a heavy surf in the middle of the street
making knees and leftovers of tenderness crash
into the the New Inn, its doors, its entrances the color of neglect.

And then the girl appeared on the balcony
standing over the afternoon that was as much hers as her room with
    its unmade bed
where every man believed he had loved her once
before forgetfulness had set in.

FROM
GOTÁN
(1962)

GOTÁN[1]

The woman was like the word never,
a special charm rose up from her neck,
a kind of forgetfulness where her eyes were safe,
the woman settled in my left side.

Watch out watch out I'd scream watch out
but she possessed me like love, like the night,
and the last signals I made that autumn
settled down quietly under the surf of her hands.

Sharp sounds exploded inside me,
rage, sadness, fell down in shreds,
the woman came down like a sweet rain
on my bones standing in the solitude.

She left me shivering like someone condemned
and I killed myself with a quick knife-thrust,
I'll spend all my death laid out with her name,
it will be the last thing to move my lips.

---

1. This word represents "tango" spelled backwards.

STUCK IN PARIS

The one I miss now is the old lion at the zoo,
we always had coffee together in the Bois de Boulogne,
he'd tell me about his adventures in Southern Rhodesia
but he made it all up, obviously he'd never been out of the Sahara.

Anyway I loved his elegance,
the way he shrugged off the little things in life,
he'd look out the café window at the French
and say "those idiots make babies."

The two or three English hunters he'd put away
stirred up unpleasant memories and even sadness,
"the things one does to keep flesh and bones together" he'd muse
admiring his mane in the café mirror.

Yes, I miss him very much,
he never picked up the bill
but would point out how much tip to leave
and the waiters saw him off with special respect.

We'd say goodbye at the approach of twilight,
he'd go back to what he called his bureau,
not before warning me with a paw on my shoulder
"watch out for the Paris night life, son."

I really miss him very much,
a desert would sometimes fill his eyes
but he knew how to be silent like a brother
moved, deeply moved when
I'd talk to him about Carlitos Gardel.[1]

---

1. Carlos (Carlitos) Gardel was and, more than thirty years after his death in a plane crash, is still the most famous singer of tangos in Argentina.

A WOMAN AND A MAN

A woman and a man swept along by life,
a woman and a man face to face
live in the night, slip over the edge of their hands,
are heard going up, free-floating in the darkness,
heads resting on a beautiful childhood
they created together, sunny, packed with light,
a man and a woman bound by their lips
fill the drawn out night with all their memories,
a man and a woman more beautiful in each other
occupy their place on earth.

THE END

A man has died and they're teaspooning up his blood,
dear john, you're dead at last.
Those pieces of you soaked in tenderness
were of no use to you.

How could you possibly get out
through a little hole
without someone to put a finger there
to keep you back?

He must have swallowed all the rage in the world
before dying
and afterwards he was so sad so very sad there
leaning on his bones.

They lowered you down, brother,
the ground trembles above you.
Let's watch and see where his hands
pushed by his immortal rage send up shoots.

FROM
COLERA BUEY
(1964–1971)

FOR THE TIME BEING

this twilight made its way in through the window the ships' masts
    motionless in it
holding still quiet to keep from disrupting the twilight
coming in to the counters at the rear of the market
where men stared into their wine getting all tangled up
hassled by women from the south
commands from their breasts like sweet alarms
the twilight in from africa the great devourer
was tying up in port with dangerous heavy movements
unloading beasts of sadness guns traps imitation ebony
the twilight lord and master
moved around the old market dealing out intimate blows
stupors of love and especially sweet disasters
faces under the influence of wine
that toward nightfall started to grow like uneasiness
like the smell of old women scrounging in garbage heaps in Santos
harbor and it was eleven o'clock in the glory of the day overhead
    but not over the greatest among those women
gentle sweet woman lost in the saliva of so many local men
torn apart devoured women old now with eyes dried up
like the evaporation of the drawn out kisses the last
spoils of darkness the old crones scrounged
for oranges rotting fish leftovers of the big show
hugging the dust greedy old women at the dancehall door
where sailors traded the sea for beerhall hookers
yarn-spinning sailors who smelled like monsters blind men dancing
    pressed up against flat breasts
where do these things happen

where do these things happen where do scraps of love drift to
    their final rest
oh how they must still echo down the ages
let me have the answer grandchildren
so cruel in your good hearts

FRIENDS

jiri wolker attila jozsef me
probably never three more perfect friends
jiri would talk about prague
and the blind stoker's eyes still fixed on us
jozsef would sing to Flora and the Revolution
and there were no trains for suicides then
or hospital beds to die in

what do you think of it? jiri jozsef me
all three knocking around going through countries and women
and drinking wine and writing brilliant poems
the world was wide and all ours we had nothing
and everything ahead of us like youth

and so this was turning out as we had always planned
in a barricade
jiri jozsef and me whistling to the end
they were giving up their bones their tremendous nevers

jiri died in a hospital
jozsef hurled himself under a train
oh god we were so beautiful
whistling to the end

HYMN OF VICTORY
(IN CERTAIN CIRCUMSTANCES)

at daybreak now in full splendor
who but me like gin destroying its beloved victims
is there to add light to the timid glow on the tables
who but me with scraps of paper rich descriptions kept to myself
and the word table the lies
the yardlengths of lies to cover up the drunkard's elbows
the tailors are sad but go on sewing and singing
fat lies are in the air brothers ugliness is beautiful
running sores loveable and infamy like great dignity
reptiles have grown on the bird distracted singer
who stares wide-eyed at their horrible sight
hurrah no one is innocent after all
ladies and gentlemen let's drink a toast virgins don't virge
bishops don't bishop functionaries don't function
everything that festers ends up as tenderness
i look at my heart swollen with losses
when there'd be so much room in it for beautiful adventures

ANOTHER MAY

when you went past my window may
with autumn on your back
and flashed signals with the light
of the last leaves

what was your message may?
why were you sad or in your sadness gentle?
i never found out but there was always
one man alone in the street among autumn's golds

well i was the boy
at the window may
shielding my eyes
when you went past

and come to think of it
i must have been the man

QUESTIONS

now that you're sailing through my blood and are familiar with my
limitations and wake me in the middle of the day to make me lie
down in your memory and push my patience too far tell me what
the devil i am doing why do i need you wordlessly coursing through
me alone you the object of my passion why do i want to fill you with
just me and encompass finish you off mingle with your bones when
you are my only country (with me) against the beasts of oblivion

FROM
JOHN WENDELL'S POEMS
(1965–1968)

XVII:
AT DAYBREAK

at daybreak
the house noises have started up again
and maybe it's ghosts or
a chest of drawers something forgotten coming apart

or it may be our kisses from the past
taking advantage of the solitude
to stop loving and collapse
and turn to dust on the floor

can it be possible?
the tiniest sound they make won't let me sleep
but I also felt lonely today
in the hallway where we tore ourselves away long ago

not from the outrage of our neighbors nor
from the african colonies nor
from the depth in the mirror but
from myself and yet you keep coming back

CCLXI:
THESE POEMS

these poems this batch of papers this
handful of fragments still trying to breathe
these soft rough words i've put together
will be the end of me

sometimes they're worse than actions or closer to the truth
time passing doesn't polish or improve them
it shows up the cracks in their flaking walls
their ceiling is caving in and it's raining

and they can give me neither shelter nor defense
i actually avoid them like cities cursed in ancient times
destroyed by plagues and disasters
by magnificent foreign kings

worse than pain are these
ruins i've built while living and letting live
moving between two waters
between this world and its beauty

and i'm not complaining for in
writing poems i sought neither gold nor glory
neither happiness nor unhappiness
neither home nor forgiveness

CIII:
I SAW MY COUNTRY'S MAP IN YELLOW ONE DAY

i saw my country's map in yellow one day
it happened suddenly and i thought how strange
the word yellow it was
a perfect day in fall

full of lives and tremors i
saw
my country floating
on the Atlantic we

were drifting along with it i felt
something like terror
or love or grief
as i faced the yellow map i thought

about my country we were all drifting
to the south the interior the north and so
i dreamt about your love
my darkened one i mean peace

fall was just beginning my country
was drifting on the sea
the wide open ocean
strange words oh so strange

FROM
DOM PERO'S POEMS
(1965–1968)

CDLXXXI:
IN A RIVER FIVE LEAGUES WIDE AT ITS
NARROWEST POINT

in a river five leagues wide at its narrowest point
and in viper or snake or serpent
the same danger of death exists
in these Indies one never knows

one never knows if the way out should have been
to push into the forests like hungry wolves
ax rifle or
machine gun in our grip

oh! the days bring on so many needs
and even more the months the years of this mortal life
and so having a snake or viper close and killing it
is eating better than King

right, fellow countrymen? blond King eat golden
pheasant in him kingdom of gold
but it don't really matter
none of it really matters

except our misery
three ounces of pain is not the same as two
many days were we stranded with such fierce passion in the cards
like animals of this land

oh Indies stranded in the South!
there was so much concern in your face
while in irons as well as in other things and in deliverance
paddling and rowing for instance and dying like animals

vassals kiss their lord's Royal feet
for free men there aren't even feet to kiss
such is the hopeless condition
of catfish monkeys tigers under the sun

but nobody complains
in these Indies nobody complains
a heavy yellow silence covered the sky
like mud the day before yesterday

ah tomorrow! tomorrow!

FROM
YAMANOCUCHI'S POEMS
(1968)

IV:
THE SUN ON THE DAY'S CREST

the sun on the day's crest gilds
points of land flags barrier reefs someone
sitting at the roadside inspects
his feet

tied down to the road he thinks
of kings swallowed up by time he sticks
a yellowed fingernail
into the sole of his right foot digs out

the tiny splinter
that made him bleed
and
feel the road under him he sniffs

at the hard sharp object still warm
his body would not accept it
dark covered with blood
and he's silent out there in the sun

XVI:
HE WAS BORN ON THE
BRINK OF A DISASTROUS DAY

he was born on the brink of a disastrous day
face to face with another just like it but
in the split or opening between the two
he had a kind of warm feeling so

he saw happiness
as a sudden break
in the heart of those identical
doomed barren painful times

when his life was snuffed out
his eyes were soft with subdued anger
or were falling like autumn leaves
in hard transparent sheets

that toured the world
and toured the heart
yet no one breathed a word
to sergeant MacIntire about this

XX:
THOSE WHO CREATED GOD

those who created god with
one or two men or
converted man into god were
punished with eternity while

those who started off
by naming the fear of death accepting
the sudden or terrifying end
(not as fury oblivion or limit) and

regarded their neck as something relative
their shoulder something temporary their
ribcage something borrowed those were
dispersed through time and history

scattered on earth like seed planted
in the sun heavy with solitude
or indecision and buried in thought
before the graveyards of white birds

FROM
SIDNEY WEST'S POEMS
(1968–1969)

Is translation betrayal?

    Is poetry translation?

—Po I-po

LAMENT FOR GALLAGHER BENTHAM

when gallagher bentham died
a strange thing happened:
the local women's hatred grew as if the price of potatoes
    had gone up
fierce harpies they started smearing his memory
as if it were gallagher bentham's duty obligation or job
to be immortal

since he took extreme care
not to anger the gods by leading a model life
he never made it a point to be good he sinned
half-heartedly and lived it up like the thousand devils
that no doubt possessed him at night
and forced him to write sacrilegious verses
in detriment of his soul

and so
he grew famous for his impertinence and his passes at women
who told their kids "there goes gallagher bentham the damn
    bastard" pointing a finger at him
but at night he filled their dreams
at night a strange lump or hand or silky feeling
crept into their throats as they dreamed of him
ah gallagher bentham father extraordinaire!
he'd have founded whole nations with his children alone
if he'd felt like fathering them
if it hadn't been for his poems
that don't beg for bread and it's one of the few things in their favor
well he died just like that and people

who were upset by the lack of morality of this immoral man
or felt that they had lost some of their freedom
appointed go-betweens to interview gallagher bentham
but no matter how many questions they threw at him
all they heard was bees humming in his body
as if he were making honey
or more poems always up to something else

it's hard to tell why his Spoker Hill neighbors got to hate him so
one morning in fall they tore him to pieces much to their children's
    delight
there were no more lumps in any woman's throat
and no fierce getting even in bed with a stray husband
not even dreams that filled the night of the more delicate women
and made the wind whirl and made it rain
all the trees in Spoker Hill dried up
but not the royal horsefly whizzing
around gallagher bentham or the last of the honey left in him

LAMENT FOR BUTCH BUTCHANAM'S TURTLE DOVE

poor butch butchanam spent his last years
caring for a blind turtle dove not wanting to see anyone
in empathy with the bird he loved and cared for
and sometimes it beat its wings on his shoulder letting fall
a sweet sound of blue orange trees whirling through the sky
of demons standing on a mouse
of stone monkeys surprised in the act of doing it

"oh turtle dove" butch would say "you love blindness
and so i've converted my heart into blindness
to let you fly around it and stay here"
but whatever has to disappear
everything one chews eats sucks drinks or tastes
would come with twilight and sadness for butch
sadness for butch

who:
dreamed about the desert planted with the skulls of cows
castles of instant sand or dust quickly settling on the ground
wave after wave (like a serpent's) of time in Melody Spring
and ancestors who no longer knew pain not even the pain of death
and spoke a slow cheerful yellow language
like a gold band around someone's neck

night after night butch butchanam dreamed
until he realized he was about to die
he made his bed face the south and lay down with his back to the sky
and on the turtle dove he left in writing a message that he was to be

buried with his back to the sky
and he lies here with his back to the sky looking at everything that
    falls and rises again
in Melody a town of wretches who:

slashed the turtle dove's throat roasted and ate it
to discover with christian horror
that it was looking up at them from the plate
with memory in its eyes

FROM
RELATIONSHIPS
(BUENO AIRES, 1971–1973)

Thus if perhaps fortitude is in the habit
of taking over the functions of ingenuity and
making up for the defects of ability, where
may the truth be more clearly seen than when
where it is explained in the simplest way?
We must immerse words in reality
till we make them hallucinate like it.
—Don José de Pellicer, Lord of Tovar, Aragonese scholar

SNOWS

his woman has come away sadder these days
her soft hands are rougher and her eyes
warmer but not as bright and the first snow
has settled on her hair as if it snowed here

the woman sheds parts of herself
and they start to burn creasing the skin
on her forehead and around her mouth
she crackles in the sun's fire

with these sounds the woman fills her bed at night
and with animals broken in yet not tame only gentle
they lead to any part of the world
they cross the night going to any part of the world

she has grown sadder these days
her soft hands are rougher and her eyes
warmer but not as bright and the first snow
has settled on her hair

RECOGNITIONS

the bars of the paddy wagon's window
cut the afternoon in two parts
the bar on the left cuts out streets trees
the one on the right cuts out feet that are far off

outside someone looking at the weak
glow behind the paddy wagon's bars thinks
"one of them is most likely a comrade" he thinks
one is most likely a comrade

this afternoon the paddy wagon's siren spins someone inside
looking at the feet cut out thinks
"one of them is most likely a comrade" he thinks
one is most likely a comrade

such encounters such
thoughts occur
on the afternoon cut in two parts
by the bars of the paddy wagon's window

REDS

rain beats down on Río de la Plata and it's going on
36 years since they killed Federico García Lorca but
what is the connection between the reality out there
and the reality in here? or
what is the connection between the unreality out there
and the reality in here?

I don't know if the river's gray line
is like the knife used to slash the sky
the knife used now to cut short children's lives in Azul
they cut short children's lives in Santa Fe and other parts of the
    republic
sometimes forever or always forever
it's one of our country's crosses

that's a fact in the West
the sun doesn't turn sunsets red here
the blood of children turns the republic's sunsets red
children in Salta in Tucumán little angels
whose lost or spilled blood is swept away by sunsets
day after day after day

and what has it to do with Federico García Lorca's death
with Federico García Lorca's execution in Granada in 1936?
or do sunsets in the West of Spain
turn red not with the sun
but with Federico García Lorca the poet's blood
day after day after day?

I don't know I don't know
"you'll fall into the river, kid!" Federico García Lorca said
"I understood when he disappeared into the water" Federico García
    Lorca said
"there's another river in the rose" Federico García Lorca said
but why does his blood turn Granada red
day after day?

and why do children in Azul Santa Fe Tucumán Salta
turn red the republic's sky
under which others forgot or pretend to forget them?
why did they fall into the river and disappear
into the water leaving squalid poverty
for the river of another rose?

what's the connection between the reality
out there and this unreality in here? or
what's the connection between the unreality out there
and this reality in here?
when did they kill Federico García Lorca in Tucumán?
when did they shoot him in Azul Santa Fe Salta?

COURAGE

the sadness a man and a woman can build up between them is
    enormous
like those two birds pecking at each other on that branch
and enormous with the rains seen in its face
is the tree itself out there in the sun

will it or won't it rain? will those
same little birds sing? will the enormous
sadness welling up growing like a lake or a sea
between a man and a woman go on and on?

will sadness fly from tree to tree?
like footsteps all alone in a room?
like coral through the air?
like planks like bridges lonely and no longer loved?

a twig has dropped into the lake and sails out
the sadness a man and a woman can build up between them is
    enormous
like the little twig's sailing across the lake
soaked to the bone with its own courage

FROM
FACTS
(BUENOS AIRES–ROME, 1974–1978)

FACTS

while the current dictator or bureaucrat was speaking
in defense of the regime's legally established disorder
he took a line or verse born of the cross
between a stone and a bright glow in autumn

outside the class struggle raged on / brutal
capitalism / back-breaking work / stupidity /
repression / death / police sirens splitting
the night / he took the line of poetry and

deftly opened it in half packing
more beauty into one part and then more
into the other / he closed up the line / put
his finger on its first word / squeezed

it aiming at the dictator or bureaucrat
the line shot out / the speech went on / the
class struggle went on / brutal
capitalism / back-breaking work / stupidity / repression / death /
    police sirens splitting the night

this explains why so far no line of poetry has overthrown
any dictator or bureaucrat not even
a small dictator or bureaucrat / and also explains
how a verse can be born from the cross between a stone and a bright
    glow in autumn or

a cross between the rain and a ship and also from
other crossings no one would know how to predict / in other words
births / marriages / the
shots fired by neverending beauty

TIME SCHEDULES

august went off arm in arm with the hydrangeas
and poetry has now settled down to work
regardless of the hot sunday
stretched out over the houses / quietly

transparent in her backdrop of light one she-bird doesn't sing/ one
tree doesn't grow at the root of its silence / and
yet poetry
has seen august arm in arm with the hydrangeas and

has settled down to work breaking
the siesta's contracts / ah lady who knows
why they picture you as someone peaceful when you may be
wearing leather aprons / must be sweating / must have

callouses from hammering verbs together or
driving off hatreds betrayals saving
the heart's clarity / lady
seen in the thick of the fight

caring for the combatant / his childhood
surrounded by gunpowder or casualties / worker
the enemy cannot carry off / surrogate
for these embraces / these lives

THINGS THEY DON'T KNOW

dark times / filled with light / the sun
spreads sunlight over the city split
by sudden sirens / the police hunt goes on / night falls and we'll
make love under this roof / our eighth

in one month / they know almost everything about us / except
this plaster ceiling we make love
under / and they also know nothing about
the rundown pine furniture under the last ceiling / or

about the window the night pounded on while you shone like the
   sun / or
about the beds or the floor where
we made love this month / with faces around us like the sun
spreading sunlight over the city

DEATHS

one day i watched death going by / she wasn't on horseback / she
    was screaming
like the swallows circling santa maria maggiore / such
a death is sad / i really mean it and in case
anyone doesn't know that such a death is sad

this one was screaming like one of the damned / of no help to her
the lovely summer the fountains the women she allowed to go on
    their way
like heat fire or pity / this death
wouldn't be worth a plugged nickel anywhere

to start off no one needed her / she wasn't bold or brave / couldn't
sing / couldn't make anyone else sing / she wasn't wearing blue
    stockings / her eyes
screamed like swallows slicing the afternoon around
santa maria maggiore / i'm telling it the way i saw it / this

death drew pity or compassion from coachmen gentle
horses in broad daylight / a death with such poor taste / alone /
    unhappy / old death / unable
to fly / without a string around her small feet / screaming
in the middle of the public square

when she had gone by i felt scared
i never want to see that death again
cross my heart i never want to see her again
especially not on the day of my death

FROM
NOTES
(CALELLA DE LA COSTA–PARIS,
ROME, AUGUST-OCTOBER 1979)

To Eduardo Galeano

To Helena

NOTE III

walking on my bare knees
through a field of broken glass /
walking on my naked soul
through a field of broken comrades /

whom neither the twilight nor the sea
that washes over any man will wash /
i don't know what's washing over them now /
quiet at last / unafraid

of death / killed /
by bullets or cyanide / by
their own or another's hand / dead
all the same / rotting

under the earth in this land
that took them in / fires
put out by military hatred / urge
us on to victory sons

NOTE V

don't keep sadness away from the fireside /
sit here beside me / old gal /
you're never going to leave me /
forgive me for neglecting you

for drifting from rage to rage
going out of one dead man entering
another dead man or shattered world /
for traveling like this all these years /

move up closer to me / sadness / so
much anger and so many dead ports
send a chill through me but
i have to go on moving / on and on

NOTE XIII

To Juan Carlos Cedrón

every comrade owned a piece of the sun /
in his soul / his heart / his memory /
every comrade owned a piece of the sun /
that's what i'm talking about

i'm not talking of the errors that
led to our defeat / for now / or
of the arrogance / blindness / insanity of the military command /
i'm saying that each comrade owned a piece of the sun

that lit up his face /
kept him warm in the terror at night /
made him beautiful lighting up his eyes /
letting him fly / fly / fly /

have those pieces of sun gone out? / with our comrades dead / have
their pieces of sun gone out? / don't they still light up their souls /
memory / heart / and warm their heels /
their bones shot through with darkness?

little sunlight you went out like that /
but you still light up this night /
while we look at that side
where the sun comes up

FROM
OPEN LETTER
(PARIS, ROME, JANUARY 1980)

To my son

IV:
CRESTFALLEN MY BURNING SOUL

crestfallen my burning soul
dips a finger in your name / scrawls
your name on the night's walls /
it's no use / it bleeds dangerously /

soul to soul it looks at you / becomes a child /
opens its breast to take you in /
protect you / reunite you / undie you /
your little shoe stepping on the

world's suffering softening it /
trampled brightness / undone water
this way you speak / crackle / burn / and love /
you give me your nevers just like a child

XVI:
PUNISHING LOVES

punishing loves / keeping sorrows down /
from sun to moonlight i pass / creatures
like living proofs of you / you may have seen them
often / now that they come around here dressed

like you / in other words beautiful / gentle like
when you looked sadly at the close of day /
and wanted not to sleep but to dream /
tugging at the night with two little fists

XX:
EARLY ON THE SOUL BEGINS TO HURT

Early on the soul begins to hurt / pale /
in the wavering light it explores your not being here /
the heart rises with misgivings /
goes over the sky like the sun

in daylong search / day in day out / it burns
freezing / as if its bones thrown out
of joint / or like an unsaid word
where i try to march against death /

soul you harmonize harmonies that barely
make it across the world's width /
broken / it broods over
what you left me / night on its feet

on August 25, 1976
my son marcelo ariel and
his pregnant wife claudia
were kidnapped in
buenos aires by a
military commando,
like in tens of thousands
of other cases, the military
dictatorship never officially
acknowledged these who
"disappeared," it referred to
"those absent forever."
until i see their bodies
or their killers, i'll never
give them up for dead.

FROM
IF GENTLY
(ROME, JANUARY-MARCH 1980)

To Juan Carlos Cedrón

IF GENTLY

if waves from someone who threw himself into the sea
came to mind gently / what about our brothers who were
in-earthed? / do leaves sprout from their fingers? /
saplings / autumns soundlessly losing their leaves? / silently

our brothers talk about the time when
they were twothree inches away from death / they smile
remembering / even now feeling their relief
as if they hadn't died / as if

paco were still brilliant and rodolfo were looking
up all the lost thoughts he'd always carried
slung over his shoulder / or rodolfo (forever) digging through
    his bitterness
had just pulled out the ace of spades / he turned his mouth to the
    wind /

inhaled life / lives / saw with his own eyes the angel of death /
but now they're talking about when
things worked out / nobody killed / nobody got killed / they
outwitted the enemy making up for some of the general
    humiliation /

with brave actions / with dreams / and all this time
their companions lying there / wordless /
flesh falling from their bones on a january night /
quiet at last / so terribly alone / without kisses

QUIET AT LAST

quiet at last / so terribly alone / without kisses / my comrades
think *me* night after night / they toss and turn
unable to sleep / restless under sheets
of earth or water where they're going away /

gone / eaten away by the truth / i toss and turn /
around this shame like a wing / fly
little bird / fly / my son's face in the middle
of my woman or loneliness / pull away /

i'm burning with the fire you burn
lowered / comrades / or neighborhoods of fire
my soul passed through like a voice
walking now with the world's feet

WALKING NOW

walking now with the world's feet / i'd ask
where do our comrades' rivers of passion
run / what seas do they burn / poor things they've simply died /
time climbed onto their shoulders to go on / they

carried winds / rages / history / they were open
to love's greatest adventure / never forgetting love itself
or self-respect / pride or dignity / if need be /
they weren't gods only men and women who

had to eat / empty their bladders / live /
procreate in the course of the physical as well as the other night /
they weren't by any means perfect / most knew nothing
about the rules of dialectic materialism / hadn't read

das kapital / their tongues tripped on economics /
but light fell from their sweating / red / wrinkled foreheads /
    thinking
of how to defeat the enemy / or help / in any case /
the air around them / the grace

that had no fear of death / unique grace / environs
of awareness of feeling / of suffering / not only one's own
but the pain of many / that rare bird singing
in the middle of the soul / wings beating

in the dark / strong / bringing exteriors
inside / or bloods like incandescences /
marvels of the other like an extension of one's soul /
running toward the sea / with light / with other souls

ALONE

you're alone / my country / without
the comrades you lock up and destroy / you hear
them slowly being emptied of the love
they have left / they loosen their grip

on their turn to die / dream they're being dreamed / quieted /
they'll never see other faces growing /
leaning out / continued / in this sun /
some day in the sun of justice

FROM
COMMENTARIES
(ROME, MADRID, PARIS, ZÜRICH, GENEVA, CALELLA DE LA COSTA, 1978-1979)

To my country

COMMENTARY I
(saint theresa)

dear love going away like a bird
stretched out over the horizons is it right
to give ourselves to the whole / without
being a part of anything / not even of the flight

that takes you away? / do sisters and brothers think
flying in circles gets you anywhere / or that
going away and at the same time staying you reach
the oneness looked for like manna from heaven?

in other words / life is difficult i mean
the health i undermine to find you like light /
or word / twig where you may rest
like your hand on my heart

COMMENTARY II
(saint theresa)

with my love running over and spilling/
all around me the miniscule animals
grow fat feeding on your absence/
or is it your presence

makes me childish like feet crushing
sadnesses on the edge of what it is about to sing/
like a magnificent victory where
my souls are reflections of you?

COMMENTARY III
(saint theresa)

clay / glass / stone / let everything
fall into place be still or wall itself in / and nothing
leave obstacle or memory / and no one
do anything except lock

all doors but one
to let love / in /
like warmth or light /
against mud and degradation /

or like shelter / like night when
suns dazzle / or light
when day blows out / or like
desired desire / even when

nothing else comes in / not even
i come in to hang around
like idle work / like sorrow
so comely on you

COMMENTARY IV
(saint theresa)

and with many birds and their songs in the /
highest part of the mind or head / and rumblings
in it like the sea / or laments /
or winds or movements / suns

that clash / go out / then burn again / or powers
like thousands of animals that track
up the suburbs of the soul / suffering
terrible ordeals i mean / even so

the soul goes on whole in its quiet state /
or desire / or clear light untouched
by sorrow / scorn / misery /
suffering or ruin / so

what is this peace without vengeance / or memory
of a future heaven / or tenderness
coming down from your hands / spring water
where birds in the highest part of the mind

rally to drink / sing sweetly / or are silent
like light issuing from you / wing
flying softly above war and fatigue
like the flight of passion itself?

COMMENTARY VII
(saint theresa)

we know / what differences there are between
rapture / tenderness / and pleasures / of the heart /
for it's one thing not to offend or hurt /
another is the delicate beauty that sobs

at the root of our happiness / and another
the one that grants favors / what's hard
to understand are the tears i shed
far from you / from your sufferings / your beauty /

your dangerous kindness / lady
who flies or returns like a shadow over my heart /
or like a sun over my sorrows
to let them rest at night

COMMENTARY XI
(hadewijch)

this longing to be alone with you / love
that makes the soul its prisoner / love
that feeds and devours and spreads the soul / wing
from you to me / taking

you far from me / love that comes and goes
with pain from you / sorrow from you / sweetness
that bathes fragments of me / united
in pleasure of you / where my exiles

away from you sing like summers/
fatherland or fever / twig
stirring up sadnesses and delights / love
like a child with closed eyes

wrapped in his own courage / or free
in the prison of you / beautiful love
offering its love to let love know
love through love itself

COMMENTARY XVII

up on a branch / high on the branch /
a flower glows / neglected? / never
reached? / lonely? / sad? / a flower
high on that branch shines

like a beacon or glory / a reminder /
of you / tenderness or flame
where exiles crackle / fire throwing
light on your faces /

or daybreaks where you fly like names
away from you / high on that branch /
neglected? / never reached? /
are you shining? / burning? / saying my name?

COMMENTARY XIX

telling the story of our darkness we take in
life clearly / the smell of damp earth
rising from your hand / where
i plant my heart without expecting

tree or reward / only
the joy of encounter or childhood
going from blood to blood / or light
that should rise up from

strolling musicians singers absorbed
in your prodigy or hand resting
on earth like warmth / or sun
coming up in the city

over punished animals /
sufferings / sorrows /
trembling silently
against the rest of the world

COMMENTARY XX

they took a man and said
turn him away but don't let him die / they picked up
this man's heart and dashed it
against the world or grief

where it burned for a while
died out and didn't come back to life as a little dog / i mean
didn't wag its tail after
its scuffle with night / and didn't look up /

or say goodbye / or turn green /
or write anything in the air /
or split like a tree /
and wasn't transformed into amber / no /

it provided no shade / no green weeds sprang up around it /
nor did they use one bone to play the flute /
and the only music it gave out
was its sadness crackling /

sadness big as an animal /
like your absence / like skies
where birds flew past
trembling in the sunlight

COMMENTARY XXVIII
(saint john of the cross)

many ways of remembering rise
from you / intimate waves /
or movements like worlds
spinning toward you / in you / all yours /

earth of you I walk upon / my self
stretched out like a tiny root
your memory shelters from
the danger of the night's animals

when distant stranger to yourself
you crackle / from you to you /
or dream yourself into my memory
that dreams remembering you /

or else i recognize your face
like memory in every face like
radiance from you / like a look in your eyes
where i see myself remembered

COMMENTARY XXXVII

the old man goes naked
to your risen love on the day
you come out into view and speak /
slender one with breasts full-blown

not looking vulnerable
but more like dawns / like tablets
of cedar where ecstatic love
defends his bride like

a wall of peace or herbs where
your lips are like two breasts
or doors where you come in to me
like perfection / like light /

like heat where my hands crackle
hands autumn is now letting fall
like leaves covered with
bright moonlight or like pure

voices in mid-flight / birds
like these regrets / these sorrows /
of mine you crush underfoot like truth
letting my anger break loose

COMMENTARY LXIII
(van gogh)

like writing letters to the
silence / asking will
misery never ever
end? / or ever be cut off

by a knife / a flash of light / a seagull
crossing it like a sky /
opening the air to let
your visitation in /

gentle you / untouched by pain /
or what is suffered by the natural /
animal unaccustomed /
to the touch of your grandeur?

FROM
CITATIONS
(ROME, NOVEMBER–DECEMBER 1979)

some of these poems are dedicated to

eduardo galeano

luisa rinser

juan carlos cedrón

elba izarduy

paco ibañez

jorge cedrón

jorge enrique adoum

To my country

CITATION I
(saint theresa)

the soul flooded with this softness / as if the whole
man / interior and exterior / drifted into oneness
and the softness were emptied
into the marrow of all the bones

that carry us around / for better / for worse / this life
you live within me / the marrow you
silently speak to me like my country
or penetrating fragrance so subtle

no one can place it / drunken feeling
that makes no effort / to love / or plead / only
to kiss me with your mouth's kisses
flooding through me / as we look into each other's eyes /

for what am i without you / except disasters? / where
will i end up if i stray from you? / so compassionate /
my one good / a sun sunning /
drying up unrequited love the want of

CITATION IV
(saint theresa)

breast or sweetness flying
over this corner where i sleep
locked in you / with you / to you / radiant soul
where i was welcomed to the light

or purity so great in its sadness /
or bird emerging from itself like
a soul burning there /
at the center of your glance /

CITATION VI
(saint theresa)

soul like a runaway horse panting /
in the middle of my thoughts / of life
itself / where is the fodder
to make your wild hooves stop? / longing

to spill so much love
and cover the bride so she can sleep
who shivers at dawn in the shadow
of your meditation? / do you smell the blossoms

in love's apple tree growing
where my many souls were lost
to let you ensoul my liberated face

with her now open halfway into herself /
beauty coming from you like prayers
where my silence wakes up suffering at dawn?

CITATION XV
(saint theresa)

in this place there is a lady /
your soul setting fire to my sweet
memory of you / like a wild
animal racing against death /

happily I survive on light /
like an open segment of passion /
or some difference in the light burning
from you to me / turtledove bringing peace /

flesh i loved beyond hope / thought
from you to you / remembering you
against the fear of knowing ourselves alive
in this dark wilderness / of sand

CITATION XXXV
(saint theresa)

soul about to leave your body /loving it /
telling it it must die / if
one has to die / go make up for its fears /
dwell on its second chances / let it know

how to burn with love and fly /
gentled by fire / beyond reach
of these miseries / these sufferings /
these remnants of pain / these

tiny pieces of you crackling in
the burning night / these small fragments /
hobbled by too many fetters to be
able to fly as much as you'd like

FROM
UNDER FOREIGN RAIN
(FOOTNOTES TO A DEFEAT)
(ROME, MAY 1980)

I write on a subject no one likes.
Not even I.
There are subjects no one likes.
—Po I-po

Earth is earth, clay is clay and the
potter works earth and clay.
That's how he knows the beauty of his
hands that are earth and clay.
—Pingala

I

It's difficult to reconstruct what happened, the truth in one's memory fights the memory of the truth. Years have gone by, the dead and the hatreds go on piling up, exile is a cow that can yield poisoned milk, apparently some persons at least thrive on it.

In Argentina's exiled colony, political as well as another kind of apathy prevail. You work or you don't, you study or you don't, you learn or don't learn the language of the country you are in, you either rebuild your life or you don't. Women pass along like rivers, you love them or you don't, you stick with them or you don't.

The need to destroy yourself and the need to survive fight each other like two brothers who've gone out of their minds. We hang up the soul's clothes in the closet but we haven't unpacked all its bags. Time passes and the way to deny exile is to deny the country we're in, its people, its language, to reject them as specific witnesses of a mutilation: our own country is far away, what do these gringos know about its voices, its birds, its mourning, its storms.

They're very different from us. They're not really concerned about us. They're not going through the injustices done to us.

Those who care most feel something like embarrassment for us. That's their problem but it affects us. As if the dialogue between foreigners about something apparently understandable—the pain others suffer—were wrapped by the others in modesty, frankness, paternalism, uses.

We'll never reach common ground. And we'll often be unjust, interpreting humility as arrogance, reserve as a lack of commitment, the will not to offend as the will not to be involved.

That's how sick we are. For affinities we'll look to the Prado Museum, Santa María Maggiore, the Place de la Contrescarpe, the Paseo de la Reforma, the escalators in Caracas, and to London's

Hyde Park. They're unreasonable affinities and last for an unreasonable length of time. The wonder passes, the pain stays. Like the soul's fire, it stays.

It stays.

Isn't this the same sky? It's not the same. Where's the Southern Cross, if not in the South? Isn't this the same sun? No.

Does it shine on Buenos Aires? It does hours later, when I'm not there anymore. A sky of a different color, foreign rain, light my childhood doesn't recognize.

The voices of the dew are like the voices of the dew. Distance, like a small tongue, samples them and tells them apart. My dew in the South or comet's tail or crystalline dawn over the breasts of the combat. The dew doesn't fall exactly the same on the European Common Market, the most common of all markets.

All men are human and what finds room in me should find it in others. And vice versa, because all men are human. Let's find room in one another, humans. Let the strange world around me with its justifiable egotisms, its parking meter-like decency, its consumer honesty, its refined brutal individualism, its pathetic love, and the filth from its hygiene all find room in me. I can merely offer it the rays that light up the fight for happiness, the generosities of death, in other words, of life, the explosions of happiness, this temporary defeat.

Let's plow the earth with our hands working together. Perhaps a plant with two faces will come up, one that needs water for both, and looks in two directions from the same solitude. This way we'll really be together.

II

What we can learn in exile is given to us, it's given to itself and buried in itself, turned inward, coiled around itself, sunk into itself, and that's not us. Can we learn something from it? Yes, we can, but what? Faces go by, turning sideways on their necks, that's something we can see. We can imagine, dream, perceive intuitively. We imagine and at the same time dream, intuit. Those cultures aren't handed to us open. Is it worth the trouble to strain ourselves, open them, force our way in, if need be? Would we find anything but the confirmation of what they did to us centuries ago and have gone on doing since? Do we have time for that?

What about the time our dead, our living ones need?

But we do have time, time not to lose our minds, not to become others. To open the fields of madness for those necks that crazily enough don't see us, lean on us to look at themselves, don't need us but are forever looking into their mirrors, chasing after themselves in the dark, with their backs turned on themselves. They come to us when they're so lost that they need calluses, rocks, something consistent to let them go on turning. They have wills of air, the air's pendulum, here today, here tomorrow also. They are short of air.

We drag our feet along in rivers of dry blood, souls that have stuck to the earth for the sake of love, we want no other worlds but the world of freedom and we don't kick that word around because we know that, for many deaths now, they have been talking in love and not about love, they talk clearly, not about clarity, talk freely, not about freedom.

XII

My father came to America with one hand behind and the other in front to hold his trousers up. I came to Europe with one soul behind and the other in front to hold my trousers up. And yet there are differences: he went to stay, I came here meaning to return.

But are there, in fact, differences? Between the two of us we went, returned, and nobody knows yet where we're going to end up.

Papa: your skull is rotting, as a sign of the world's injustice, in the country where I was born. That's why you spoke so little. You didn't have to. As for the rest—eating, sleeping, suffering, fathering children—they were necessary, natural acts, like someone's who fills his notebook with the record of his life.

I'll never forget you, in the dining room's semi-darkness, turned toward the clear light of your origins. You talked with your country. You had never really shaken its earth from the feet of your soul. Feet full of earth like enormous silence, lead or light.

XVI

What really hurts me is our defeat.

Exiles are tenants of solitude. They may correct their memory, betray, disbelieve, conciliate, die or come out on top. In this last case, they looked at their face as if it were theirs: it was filled with traitors, disbelievers, conciliators, the dead and also those compañeros who died with faith and burn in the night and repeat their names and won't let you sleep.

To make you see the distances no one lets you sleep.

You rattle your bones, you.

So be it.

FROM
SOUTHWARD
(ROME, 1981–1982)

to juan josé
to alicia
compañeros
de partido

WHAT HAVE THEY DONE

What have they done with the day full of tigers
as soft as your skin / or crazy nests
where your dress fluttered
suggesting another song / not this one

filled with leaves or salt /
your eyes having grown like suns /
the light's lower limbs started at your feet /
and no one received letters from the void /

what have they done with the tiger
full of days / gentle ways / you /
like the trees you'd make sketches of

to give shade at night /
against this fire crackling sadly
in your eye after long thought /

YOU TASTE

you taste like salt when i kiss
the quiet sea on your skin / i hear clocks /
marking hours so unlike those
we're living here / hours that bring in the bird perched

on your voice / water bird / cloud bird /
bird lying on the sea floor / opening
the little streets the stars come down to
at night / and that's how my day starts /

each day starts like this / the stars come down
to shield our comrades' bones / to take
a cinder from a burning compañero /
the clear dream of a compañero /

to let him out / to star again / to write on the night
"juan's comrades hear the sun's noises /
the noise they make in the sun /
they're comradely / and grow quiet with the sun" /

the day starts
with a burning heart / it starts fires
in my thoughts / the elbow / the darkness
opening its eyes on your sea /

you're loved by me and compañeros lying in the south / waiting
for the stars each night / the day's adventure /

a small boy spreads his white hair over you /
woman you share out my soul around the world /

our compañeros let their courage fall like autumns /
on each small leaf they've printed a stranger's heart /
from each small leaf a comrade will rise
to tie the stars down and make you love me /

FROM
JOSÉ GALVÁN'S POEMS
(1981)

the monster of reason
engenders dreams
—Julio Greco

Note:

It's my duty to pass on these poems that reached me by chance or by a miracle. Their author disappeared toward the end of 1978 in Argentina, murdered or kidnapped by the military dictators. We knew of his imprisonments and exiles under other dictatorships and of a handful of poems he published in out-of-the-way literary magazines in the city of Buenos Aires.—Juan Gelman

RODOLFO SAID IT

memory is our graveyard /
in it we bury our closest comrades /
they had a sea on their faces and warm daydreaming flowers grew
    for them/
whose souls were not sick with human discretion /

this hand flowing there also has
the warmth of paco / of the cheek it dried once
when betrayal spilled more tears on it
than mary magdalene on christ / i spend my life

turning this hand into a graveyard /
but those tears wait with our comrades for the cool air of dawn/
having died loving they are not dead /
they ask why you're so sweet /

they remember you dressed in white /
your face covered with moonlit seas and sunny seas /
on each sea an apple tree / and in its shade /
you give out the love our comrades never had a chance to give /

you heal those whom so much desolation killed /
whose tenderness was injured / burned /
they nailed your innocence on the day's wooden planks /
a pair of tiny shoes walk through your flame or lovely light /

the heart has no feet yet moves around /
wandering through the enormous sadness /
don't you hear it pounding without respite on your lips? /
you pass along on each wave / so that no one else will die

AWAKENING

to Carmelo

those poems you wrote yesterday
are pacing up and down the room / they don't
give off the light they gave last night /
when they sat up naked / like delights to come /

they may walk on and on but they'll never reach your country /
which is this room full of your country /
a map of it is pinned to the wall /
it bids you good morning every day / the rock

where hope sits waiting is very old / yesterday's
poems are sad / you look at the map alone there
and the ocean pounding its shores / while
the leaves of the magnolia poem dry up /

the hummingbird poem doesn't fly anymore /
the stars of the sky poem have deserted it /
the love poem is feeling cold /
and

you may shiver in the room the afternoon has taken over /
and later on the night will take /
you'll pace up and down like a tiny bird
with its flight tucked under its arm /

NOW

now miguel ángel crosses our country's night /
he's riding a small fiery horse /
he's dropping words that tremble like the south /
he's firing bullets of hope /

is it true the Military's torture made you come apart? /
did you fall about in tiny pieces? / what
grows from each of these? / another ángel / miguel?
or perhaps the others? / a drifter? / a sad woman? /

an old sentiment of immortality? / saint theresa? /
the hard worker / who rode a fiery horse in order to live again each
    time? /
like the scent your soul gives off? /
pieces of this lover slipped through time's claws /

i ask these things to know how i'm doing now /
you're trapped in the middle of bullets and terrors /
your poems cross the country's night /
your tenderness works on / delicate / laborer /

you wander through plazas and streets with memory in your hand /
the first morning light stumbles in /
no one gives any quarter here /
you come apart / miguel / putting together skies /

but i remember that some day you'll return /
hanging on to the rock of your destiny /
sweeping death away from each night /
riding a small fiery horse /

NESTS

to francesco

the mouths of the comrades who landed in death
are filled with orange trees
planted in the middle of their afternoons /
trees they fed to these whenever

they fought the enemy or dreamed /
they fed them the echo and the fury of their bullets /
love's wounded turtle-dove nested in their gunfire /
the orange trees opened their branches and twilights fell out

that comrades pinned down to keep them quiet /
and let everyone hear the beauty that's still to come /
the comrades had a small portion of the beauty still to come /
they would let it fall to make everyone go out

and look for justice in the streets /
for sunlight against these cold weathers from the south /
the comrades' mouths are full of silence /
like a child without news from wherever life's head droops with sleep /
the orange trees open up like a window /
the comrades lean out to watch time pass
and transform their flesh into a bell
ringing to warn about the wind from the south /

OTHER WRITINGS

night strikes your face like God's feet /
what is this light rising from your dead? / do you see anything by
   the light of this light? / what do you see? / little bones holding
   up autumn? / someone

scratching the world's walls with his bones? / anything else? /
are they scratching the soul's walls? / writing
"long live the struggle"? / are they scratching
the night's walls? / or writing "long live the soul"? /

scratching the fire where i burned and we died / all of us
   compañeros? / are they writing? /
in the fire? / in the light? / in the light of that light? /
now our comrades are walking past with their tongues locked /
they go past with the other feet and their roads /

they are going past stitched on to the light /
they're scratching the silence with a bone /
writing down the word "struggle" /
the bone has turned into a bone that writes /

YOU

ronco

you grabbed hold of death and got her into bed /
you shook her down to the last bone /
death was going around with warmth for you in her heart /
her skull started covering itself with faces /

one face as lovely as the South talking to the river /
the other looked like my brother nailed on to autumn /
leaves fall from him like thirst into the night /
like those falling from my brothers in the southern night /

the leaves of my brothers in the south have eyes of clay /
they look at the world to turn it blue /
their hearts are like a wind
to fold around the naked night /

but i was talking of faces you made at death to force her to love /
to make her wear a kiss on her lips /
to make her be beautiful to you /
to make her love herself /

you had a child at the first light of day /
another lay sleeping on the threshold of your soul /
suddenly you were glittering with stars /
you were as quiet as the sun /

FROM
THE END
(ROME, 1981–1982)

FUOCO

there is a sadness /
sitting down on my bed to talk /
it says things that happened and things still to come /
now and then it comes up with something right / for instance /
    that you don't love me /
but it doesn't even remember when you loved me /
and we were life's favorites /
and the stars wandered through our happiness /
you were as lovely as a sun /

you'd put your small hands on my chest /
you warmed the world to spend the night in / something else
the sadness doesn't say is that you're going to love me /
that you're going to come along again /

that i'm going to hear your footsteps in this room /
i'll watch you preparing tenderness /
you'll warm my heart / like tonight
when you start a big fire

to let no one get lost looking for what it loves /
the victory we're losing sight of /
in fact / sadness / you never mention victory /
you talk of dead compañeros but never of those still alive /

you sit on my bed wearing an apron of ashes /
you're as slow as an ox /
you sing up in an iron tree
and invent sadnesses /

but i came here to talk of beauty /
it opens its childhood like an area of you /
you talk to me / you remember to forget me /
you write letters to fury /

victory will soon come along /
to welcome our living compañeros /
with suns like brothers who left their bones out in the sun /
it will open up the bed for the sun /

FROM
JULIO GRECO'S POEMS
(1981)

dialogue:

"why do you write?" a little bird said to me.

"how should I know?" I said.

"why do you ask?" I said.

"how should I know?" he said.

—yamanocuchi ando

to roberto matta

to sebastián matta

Note:

Julio Greco was killed fighting against the military dictatorship on October 24, 1976. I saved these poems of his.—José Galván, Buenos Aires, 1978

THE BEAUTY OF ALL THINGS CREATED

without a prison / or regulations to keep in mind /
my soul wanders / throwing off more sparks than
aunt adelaida when she came to terms with God /
offering Him devotions and silence sent up

in exchange for uncle luis's salvation /
aunt adelaida's skirts showed signs of distress /
many moons could have been made with the loneliness of her bed
    sheets /
but auntie was always worried about things to come /

she was scared that when she turned her soul over to mrs bones /
she'd never again see my uncle / fragrant as smoke coming from
an incense burner / or at least that's how she remembered him
back in her young skirts and sheets / where the two /

had joined bodies / in love
and delicate substance / creating another country /
beautiful / with animals that grazed on their bodies /
on herbs of sweetness sprouting from their bodies after love /

and before love /
their present was full of grace /
with one face she saw the happy moments of the past /
with the other she looked ahead to a happy future /

aunt adelaida
brings to mind colonel santos lópez /
who fought with sandino / was defeated / survived /

spent 30 years cleaning his gun with the rags of memory /

and brought it out again when carlos fonseca amador came along/
who didn't use his name in vain /
when tomás borge / silvio mayorga / el cuje / germán
    pomares / those fighting at the front arrived /
and comrade santos lópez was seen in the thick of battle /

whistling softly like two who finally meet /
because each carries in his glass the water he must drink /
but in compañero santos lópez's glass
there was room for a sea / and another sea after that /

and a love / and after that another love /
and a soul and another soul / and an eternity / and another / others /
and he knew how an eternity of waiting turns into the hope of
    victory /
and that not even victory is eternal /

the only thing eternal was aunt adelaida /
she carried on her business with God like a burning coal /
she'd get up at 5:00 a.m. / stir the cinders back to life /
put her heart on to boil /
and that's how she started her day / each day /

FROM
THAT
(PARIS, 1983–1984)

some of these poems are dedicated to

Osvaldo Bayer

Aurora Bernárdez

Arnaldo Calveira

José Martín Arancibia

José Angel Valente

Daniel Viglietti

René Zapata

RAIN

it's raining hard today, very hard,
and it looks like they're scrubbing down the world.
next door my neighbor watches it rain
and thinks of writing a love letter /
a letter to the woman who lives with him
cooks washes his clothes and makes love with him
and looks like his shadow /
my neighbor never says words of love to his woman /
he goes into the house through the window not the door /
you may go into many places through a door /
workplace, headquarters, jail,
all the buildings in the world /
but not into the world /
nor into a woman / nor into the soul /
i mean / into that box or place or rain we give that name /
like today / when it's raining hard /
and i find it difficult to write the word love /
because love is one thing and the word love something else /
and only the soul knows where the two meet /
or when / or how /
but what can the soul explain /
that's why there are storms in my neighbor's mouth /
shipwrecked words /
words that don't know the sun's out because they're born and
    die on the same night he made love /
and leave in his mind letters he'll never write /
like the silence between two roses /
or like me / writing words to get back

to my neighbor who's watching it rain /
back to the rain /
and my exiled heart /

FROM
COM/POSITIONS
(PARIS, 1984–1985)

to josé ángel valente

EXERGUE

i call the following poems com/positions because i've
com/posed them, in other words, put my own things in texts great
poets wrote centuries ago. obviously i wasn't trying to improve
them. their vision of exile shook me up and i added—or changed,
went through, offered—the things i myself felt. as contempora-
neousness or companionship? mine with theirs? the other way
around? tenants of the same condition?

in any case, i talked with them. as they did with me from the dust
of their bones and the radiance of their words. i don't know which
to honor more: the beauty of their poems or the vital voice that
composed them. but the two combine to offer me the past, surround
my present and give me a future.

such is the mystery of the human word. it has its origin, whatever
the language, in the same flight between darkness and light and
thus it consubstantiates them: its light is dark, its darkness bright.
with each tongue, with each human group it opened a mouth to
make flight possible, follow its slow movement at all times, see how
it develops and has to be worked out.

translation is something inhuman: no language or face lets itself be
translated. you have to leave one beauty intact and supply another
to go with it: their lost unity lies ahead.

that's what the tower of babel was all about: not essential discord
but a partial science of the word. reality has a thousand faces and
each, its own voice. science, but also patience to let the face and its

word rise from the fear that binds them all the way to the love that will unite them. time and its pain, like patience, burn deep into the night where each word is a cold star, a sun that is still to come.

THE DOOR

open the door / my love /
get up / open the door /
my soul cleaves to my palate
trembling with terror /

the wild boar crushed me underfoot /
the wild ass came after me /
on this midnight in exile
i myself am a beast /

—*solomon ibn gabirol*
(1021–1055, malaga-zaragoza-valencia)

FAITHLESS

she left me / went to heaven /
she of the lovely throat wrapped in a necklace /
has the sweetest lips /
but she is bitter /

swords flashed in her eyes /
lances she sharpens to kill unfortunate men /
her eyes send out signals /
she is high-strung / like a thirsty deer /

her eyebrow / or bow / or rainbow /
recalls Noah's covenant / the sign that the flood was over /
if you're thirsty /
she tells her clouds to flood your heart with broken glass /

—*solomon ibn gabirol*

THE BANISHED

they turned me out of the palace /
i didn't care /
they exiled me from my country /
i wandered over the face of the earth /
they deported me from my language /
it followed me /
you kept me away from you / and
my bones are burning out /
living flames scorch me /
i am banished from myself /

—yehuda-al-harizi
(1170–1237, toledo-provence-palestine)

THE SLEEPER

you are asleep / i am awake /
like a somnambulist I walk in circles around your sleep /
you are asleep / i cross the wilderness of rocks
that tremble at my sorrow / and i darken the moon /
you are asleep / your radiance /
robs my eyes of sleep /
you're asleep in your warmth /
i'm awake in the shivering night /
all my thoughts are watching you sleep /
they melt like wax in your flame

—*joseph tsarfati (giuseppe gallo)*
(?–1527/rome-constantinople-rome-suburbs of vicovaro)

THE PRISONER

gazelle / you're far away /
yet you're closer to my bones than even i am /
the world may think i'm a free man
yet each word from you is my mistress /
and though i may walk upright in everyone's eyes
i am the prisoner of my loneliness for you /
without father or mother / without water or bread /
i walk naked in the sun of your absence /

—*joseph tsarfati*

THE JUDGMENT

that grace time saw growing on your brow /
time will reap / and will not give it back /
and the high throne you believed so high and eternally yours /
time will lower it into the grave /
and the pain you tied me down with in your hour of victory /
time will sever with its axe and its knife /
time lowers down / time raises up /
from his no-man's land the exile will depart

—*joseph tsarfati*

THE MOMENT

she told me to cheer up /
"God granted you 50 years in this world" / she said to me / and
she doesn't know / or even suspect that /
under the tissues of my heart /
there's no difference between the days i lived /
and the olden days when Noah lived /
in this world this hour alone is mine /
this now that i am /
shows its face and
like a cloud / passes on

—*samuel hanagid*
(993–1056, cordoba-granada-the battlefield)

MOMENTS DURING THE BATTLE OF ALFUENTE

the enemy pitched its tents on the hillside /
we did it in the mountain pass /
lances flashed in the sun /
and day erupted in hatred / anger / rage /
the men were reaping the rewards of death /
the day was a blurry haze /
the sun dark as night / and my heart also /
the land reeled like a drunk /
the horses leapt into the air
swift as vipers from a nest /
what a deadly hail of javelins /
arrows rattled like rain on our shields /
the enemy's swords sparkled diamonds in the night /
men's blood spilled at every turn /
like blood of the lamb at the altar's foot /
my men laughed at life / at death /
each wound on their faces a crown /
oh young lions /
to die / they believed / is to keep the faith /
and to live without faith / they thought / against the rules /

—*samuel hanagid*

THE JASMINE

behold the jasmine /
its green leaves /
its chrysolite-green stems /
its flowers white as breasts /
its tendril red /
like a lunar woman
who spilled the blood of an
innocent man /

—samuel hanagid

INVITATION

i would give my life for her
whom harps and flutes may awaken
in the middle of the night /
to let her see me
with the goblet in my hand /
and say
"your wine is in my mouth" /
and the moon looked like a C
written in gold ink
on the night's walls /

—*samuel hanagid*

ON LEARNING THAT MY ENEMY HAD DIED

i dreamt about your death / later on
i dreamt at your death / ibn abi musa:
you fulfilled my two dreams! /
did they mutilate your body / and drag
your corpse through the streets? /
my feet dance and my hands clap /
i celebrate with apples / i rinse
the roof of my mouth / my old wound / with wine /
did they torture you / destroy
your soul with
the scraps of your mangled flesh? /
today i won't read the lamentations /
today i'll read the song of songs /
the sudden apparition of the bride /
lovely as the moon /
radiant as the sun / terrifying
as an army in battle formation /
it blots out your face / blurred / sinking /
i drink from the bride's cups /
her breasts of inexhaustible liqueur /
i kiss the wheat that grows upon her womb
with white lilies around it / while you /
ibn abi musa /
visit the stench of the tomb /
you discover the night of the pit /
you have only a hissing of serpents
for company on your way to ashes /
i am here / i put on some perfume / i adjust
my fancy clothes / i recall

the fortress in ruins
where one day i thought about the generals /
the soldiers / the builders /
the destroyers / slaves / masters /
men in power / beggars /
hired mourners / the newly wed /
parents and offspring /
who at one time bedded down
on the ground / and now bed down
under the ground / they passed
from the light above to the dust / like you /
ibn abi musa /
as i will pass /
like the hatred that bound us /
to its rages / its terrors /

—*samuel hanagid*

THE PHOENIX

i was arrogant / i believed
you were a blank page
just like your soul / i mistook
your goodness for simplicity / your simplicity
for unconcern with the world / i wrote
lines i shouldn't have / words /
in the night obsessed with me / but i
was not eyes for the blind / feet for the cripple /
i believed i was clothed in righteousness / i thought
"i'll perish in my nest and like the phoenix
i'll multiply my days" / but i was
foolish and rude / i strayed
on my way to you /
with the wall pulled down / and the door forced open /
sorrows crashed down on me /
they harass me / who am nothing now /
you left like the wind / you / whom i loved more than
                              anything /
my bones / kin
to dust and ashes /
cry out for you and you don't hear me /
i'm with you and you don't see me /
i slow my steps toward you /
i make a covenant with my eyes not to see you /
there's one last stop for me: death /

—job

WHEN

when Death makes you its prisoner /
your house / of what use will it be to you? /
it may be made of bricks /
but what use will it be? /
your uncles / your brothers / your wife /
what use will they be? /
you'll die / they
will offer you a pitcher (with cracks in it) / a mat (in shreds) /
     a shroud /
they'll drop you off at the crematorium /
and you'll be dead / their tears
will soon dry /
they won't lose their appetites /
don't forget this when you're down below
answering to Death's notary /
stripped of your clothes / will you speak up ? /
possessions or relatives will be of no use /
they
will not go with you /
whose are you? /
you won't know it either
when you melt into the final purity /
obstinate heart: you pretend not to catch on /
though you've followed close on the trail
of the poem in the water a thousand times /

—ramprasad
(1718–1775, kumarhatta-calcutta-kumarhatta)

168

FROM
ANNOUNCEMENTS
(PARIS, 1985)

tot es niens
—*Guillaume de Poitiers*

EACH TIME I GO DOWN
THE RUE DES ARTS AND APRIL

each time i go down the rue des arts and april
there's a smell of "fontanares" cigarettes
i smoked behind the execution wall / scrunched under the sky /
with hands like a nervous pagoda
shielding the faded cinders from the daylight /
and each time i go down the rue des arts
i see ana in the open lot behind the wall /
her eyes filled with april / with angry friends / eyes a
    violet hazel color/
filled with fishes / some burning like suns / others raining /
    those eyes
were like two recently pruned trees warm with birds
that had just left their wooden perch / heir to feathers
that held up the air never felling all the way / and around
    those eyes
    there was a lake the color of the pearls of mei-lan-fan /
the darling of my fears /
pearls that mei-lan-fan cultivated in her head
to let there be light on certain nights /
like today / when i stroll down april /
with my soul folded under my armpit like a student of the
                       soul /
through the city that has no eyes to see ana /
it doesn't see her fresh breasts just starting to bud
and tremble the way my seven years
of a small boy trembled once / confused
by so much naked bugle / so much glory / so much desolation /
so much sad cheer / what to be? /

those no-man's-lands no one dared listen to! /
those first fruits like thousands of legions
launched against one! /
that beauty / with me in it / without victories! /
the carts / the women / the children /
dragged from one country to the next / from your loveliness to
    my pain! /
to all the yesterdays that would pass! /
when will you prompt your kindness or your future contempt
    to come to the rue des arts /
where i once smoked "fontanares"
to put off death?

FROM
LETTER TO MY MOTHER
(GENEVA, PARIS, JULY 1984
PARIS, NOVEMBER 1987)

To Teodora

LETTER TO MY MOTHER

i received your letter 20 days after your death and
five minutes after knowing you had died /
a letter that weariness, you said, had cut
short / they had thought you looked well at the time /
sharp as ever / still spry at 85
after the three operations for the cancer
that finally took you away /

did cancer do it? / or was it my last letter? / you
read it, answered it, died / did you guess that i
was getting ready to go back? / i'd walk into
your room / and you wouldn't believe your eyes / and we'd
kiss / hug each other and cry / and
kiss again / say each other's names / and we're together again /
not in these hard irons /

you / who held off your death so long / why
couldn't you wait for me a little longer? / did you fear
for my life? / was that your way of protecting me? /
did i never grow up for you? / did some part of your
body go on living off my childhood? / is that why
you turned me away from your death? / as you had once before
from you? / because of my letter? / did you somehow know? /

we seldom wrote each other during these years of exile /
it's also true that we spoke little before then /
even as a boy, the one you brought up turned against you / and
your confining love / and i swallowed my share of rage and
sadness / you never laid a hand on me /

you whipped me with your soul / oddly enough
we were close /

. . . . .

i weighed 5.5 kilos at birth / you lay in the hospital's
hard bed for 36 hours before bringing me out
into the world / you kept me as long as your body
could / were you comfortable with me
inside you? / didn't i gradually give you fits,
palpitations, kicks, fears, hates,
pent up emotions? / were you and i okay, together like that, i
swimming in the dark in you? / what did you
tell me then with the silent strength you always had
later on? / i must have been very happy inside
you / never wanting to come out of you / you
cast me out and the castaway cast you off /

are those the ghosts i haunt myself with now /
at my age / like when i was swimming in your
water? / is that why i am so blind, so slow
finding out, as if i didn't want to, as if
the important thing were still the darkness your womb
or home pulled over me? / darkness with its infinite
gentleness? / where the brightness far off doesn't punish
with the stone-world or pain? / is it life with its eyes
closed? / is that why i write poems? / to retreat
into the womb where each word will be born? / by
a tenuous thread? / is poetry a substitute for you? / your
sorrows and your delights? / do you destroy yourself with me like the
word in the word? / is that why i write poems? /

do i destroy you this way? / you'll never be born of me? / are
words these ashes that make us one? /

you always knew what exists between us but never
told me / was i at fault? / did i blame you all this
time for casting me out of you? / is that my
real exile? / did we blame each other for that love
we sought through separations? / did it set
bonfires to light up our distance? / was each
non-encounter proof of the last encounter? /
is that how you measured infinity? /

what oblivion is ever peace? / of all your living faces
why do i recall with such detail only one
photograph? / Odessa, 1915, 18 years old,
you're studying medicine, there's nothing to eat/but
two apples had risen to your cheeks (that's how you
described it to me) (tree of hunger that yields fruit) / did those apples
    have red tints of fire from the pogrom that
had been yours? / at the age of 5? / your mother leading
several siblings from the burning house? / and your
young sister dead? / with all that / because all that /
against you / do you love me? / did you ask me to be
your small sister? / is that why you gave me this woman, / inside /
and outside of me? / what is this legacy, mother / that
photograph of you a lovely 18-year old / with long
hair as blue-black as the night of the soul / parted
in the middle / the flared dress marking your
breasts / the two girlfriends lying at your feet / your
eyes looking at me so i'd know i love you
irrevocably? /

. . . . .

and this afternoon / isn't it full of you? / of those times
when you loved me? / the voice singing at the end of the street /
    isn't it your voice? / the womb trembling with us still together? /
    what is this difficult love / so subtly
yours / rain for your fire / fire for your wood / flame
written in the fire with your last little bone / fire standing in the
    night? / high above / what are you crying out in my soul? / but
    you're not screaming at me / with your palate gone into tents of
    darkness i feel cold / how many times did you feel my shivering?
    / did you look at me astonished at yourself? wasn't i perhaps the
    worst kind of monster to you? / the one you created? / and how
    did you manage to love me? /
did you nourish that work against your own
darkness? / and when i opened my mouth, didn't you scream? /
didn't my tongue frighten your tongue? / didn't your saliva hold a
    garden of fear? / that i seeded /
cultivated / watered with my-your blood? / and what did i
kill in you when you brought me into the world? / how deep did
    my disasters go in? / and our unfinished meeting / never / ever /
    and forever again to be? / what of the stony ground
from you to you on which my knees bled? /
the times you cried next to my bed over so many things / and my
    fever/and the fever of your wild early years?/

. . . . .

through you i came to the beauty of day / through me you go
deep into the night / with your eyes withdrawn because
there was nothing more to see / but the fine sound that

178

undoes all i made you suffer / now that you're
motionless /
and what's this love of ours like / now? /
with hyacinth they'll cover the table once filled with bread /
yet there'll be no one
to speak to me / i'm tied down to your gentleness / i feed
your blindest animal /
you / to whom do you grant respite now? /
all your dresses have turned white /
the sheets smother me and i can't sleep / you
really hate yourself in me / myrrh
and incense you planted in my time have grown / let them
cover you with scent / and accompany your grace / let my soul
prepare your passing into nothingness /
i still gather lilies you must have left here
to let me see the two sides of your love /
to rock your cradle / to wash your diapers / so that you'll
never leave me again /
without warning me / without asking me /
you howled when i set you aside /
let's never have to forgive each other anymore /

FROM
THE WAGES OF THE PROFANE
(PARIS, GENEVA, MEXICO,
NEW YORK, 1984–1992)

A quick death is very light
punishment for the ungodly. You'll die
in exile, wandering, far
from your native land.
Such are the wages an ungodly man
deserves.
—Euripides

THE ANIMAL

I live with an obscure animal.
At night he eats anything I do during the day.
During the day he eats anything I do at night.
The only thing he doesn't eat is my memory. He gets a rise
from pointing out my smallest errors and fears.
I don't let him sleep.
I am his obscure animal.

COURAGE

To José Angel Valente

Word that is extinguished when we breathe or name its impossibles, bones that burned to give it shade, palate that ended in spittle; what had been body now burns out to let the horizon take form. A verse works its way into poetry and, around the world, the slimy dawn is a forest of blood. Or are those the footsteps of terrified Death? There are no more cities of refuge, Cedes, Arama, Asor have sweating brows, their swallows fled to the trees of the sun. Now everything is birth.

THE WORD

To Rigas Kappatos

The word that would name you rests in the shadows. When it names you, you will become a shadow. You'll crackle in the mouth that lost you to have you.

LIKE

You're like the granite Buddha who receives on his plate the
only gift a child could give him: a handful of dust from the
road.

YOUNG VENETIAN LADY'S DÜRER PORTRAIT REVISITED

I came back to look at the young Venetian woman who taught me
the solace of love. She's immortal and hurts me in a gentle
way. She has withdrawn to an air she'll never open to me.
Ages ago I had a dream on her lips. It is intact. She left
it there and there it remains, closed to me, whose dream it
is.

Acknowledgments from the Editor, Paul Pines:

I would like to thank Steve Luttrell, publisher/editor of the *Café Review* for his strong support of this project, and novelist/translator David Unger, whose help was crucial in bringing this book to light.

About the Author:

Juan Gelman (Buenos Aires, Argentina, 1930) is one of the most read and influential poets in the Spanish language. He published more than twenty books of poetry from 1956 onward and has been translated into fourteen languages. A political activist and critical journalist since his youth, Gelman was not only a literary paradigm, but also a moral one, within and outside Argentina. Awards he received in his lifetime include the National Poetry Prize (Argentina, 1997), the Juan Rulfo Prize in Latin American and Caribbean Literature (Mexico, 2000), the Pablo Neruda Prize (Chile, 2005), the Queen Sofia Prize in Ibero-American Poetry (Spain, 2005), and the Cervantes Prize (Spain, 2007). He died in 2014 in Mexico City.

About the Translator:

Hardie St. Martin was a master translator. In his long and distinguished career as an editor and translator, Hardie translated work by Pablo Neruda, Vincente Aleixandre, Roque Dalton, Enrique Lihn, Nicanor Parra, and Luisa Valenzuela, among others. He was the recipient of a John Simon Guggenheim fellowship in 1965, and a P.E.N. International Translation Award and an ALTA award for excellence in editing and translation. His anthology of Spanish poetry, *Roots and Wings* (1975), is still considered a literary landmark. St. Martin died in Barcelona in 2007.

O pen Letter—the University of Rochester's nonprofit, literary translation press—is one of only a handful of publishing houses dedicated to increasing access to world literature for English readers. Publishing ten titles in translation each year, Open Letter searches for works that are extraordinary and influential, works that we hope will become the classics of tomorrow.

Making world literature available in English is crucial to opening our cultural borders, and its availability plays a vital role in maintaining a healthy and vibrant book culture. Open Letter strives to cultivate an audience for these works by helping readers discover imaginative, stunning works of fiction and poetry and by creating a constellation of international writing that is engaging, stimulating, and enduring.

Current and forthcoming titles from Open Letter include works from Bulgaria, Catalonia, China, Germany, Iceland, South Africa, and many other countries.

www.openletterbooks.org

CPSIA information can be obtained
at www.ICGtesting.com
Printed in the USA
JSHW020953110123
36119JS00003B/10